Free Surname

Ireland: 1600s to 1900s

From Ireland Church Records of Baptism, Marriage and Death

Comprised of Roman Catholic and Church of Ireland Records

From Counties Carlow, Cork, Kerry and Dublin City

Compiled by **Donovan Hurst**

February 26, 2013

ISBN: 1939958016
ISBN-13: 978-1-939958-01-3

Dedication

This work is dedicated to all of those that came before us and shaped our lives to make us the people that we are today.

Table of Contents

Introduction

This is a compilation of individuals who have the surname of Free that lived in the country of Ireland from the 1600s to the 1900s. I have placed each entry into one of four categories: Families, Individual Births/Baptisms, Individual Burials, and Individual Marriages. If a marriage entry primarily concerns an Individual Free whom is female, then I have placed that entry under the category of Individual Marriages. If a marriage entry primarily concerns an Individual Free whom is male, then I have placed that entry under the category of Families. Images of many of these listings are available at http://churchrecords.irishgenealogy.ie/churchrecords/.

To help guide the reader of this work, the format of this book is as follows:

- Main Family Entry (Husband and Wife) (Father and Mother)

  o Child of Main Family Entry, including Spouse(s) when available

    ▪ Grandchild of Main Family Entry, including Spouse(s) when available

      • Great-Grandchild of Main Family Entry, including Spouse(s) when available

(**Bolded Text**) following any entry includes any additional information such as Residence(s), Occupation(s), Signature(s), etc. when available.

Hurst

Some of the fonts used in this work symbolizes Celtic writing. The traditional letters, numbers, and punctuation marks and their Celtic counterparts are as follows:

Traditional Letters (Uppercase & Lowercase)

A a B b C c D d E f G g H h I i J j K k L l M m N n O o P p Q q R r S s T t U u V v W w X x Y y Z z

Celtic Letters (Uppercase & Lowercase)

A a B b C c D ð E e F f G g H h I í J j K k L l M m

N n O o P p Q q R r S s T t U u V v W w X x Y y Z z

Traditional Numbers

1 2 3 4 5 6 7 8 9 10

Celtic Numbers

1 2 3 4 5 6 7 8 9 10

Traditional Punctuation

. , : ' " & - ( )

Celtic Punctuation

. , : ' " & - ( )

Free Surname Ireland: 1600s to 1900s

Parish Churches

Carlow (Church of Ireland)

Aghold Parish, Carlow Parish, Cloydagh Parish, Killeshin Parish, Painestown Parish, Staplestown Parish, and Tullow Parish.

Dublin (Church of Ireland)

Clondalkin Parish, Rathmines Parish, St. Bride Parish, St. Catherine Parish, St. George Parish, St. James Parish, St. Luke Parish, St. Mark Parish, St. Mary Parish, St. Nicholas Without Parish, St. Paul Parish, St. Peter Parish, St. Thomas Parish, and St. Werburgh Parish.

Dublin (Roman Catholic or RC)

Lucan Parish, Rathmines Parish, SS. Michael & John Parish, St. Agatha Parish, St. Andrew Parish, St. Audoen Parish, St. Catherine Parish, St. Mary Parish, St. Mary, Donnybrook Parish, St. Mary, Pro Cathedral Parish, St. Michan Parish, and St. Nicholas Parish.

Kerry (Church of Ireland)

Dingle Parish and Tralee Parish.

Families

- Annesley Free & Unknown

  o William Annesley Free & Sophia Wyse – 9 Nov 1879 (Marriage, **Rathmines Parish**)

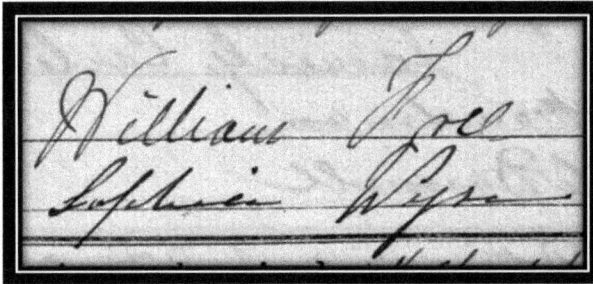

Signatures:

- Annesley Hamilton Free – b. 30 Aug 1880, bapt. 23 Sep 1880 (Baptism, **St. Peter Parish**)

- Charlotte Mary Free – b. 14 Sep 1882, bapt. 24 Oct 1882 (Baptism, **St. Peter Parish**)

- Richard Oustangue Free – bapt. 25 Nov 1885 (Baptism, **St. Peter Parish**)

- Sophia Evelyn Free – b. 16 Mar 1887, bapt. 19 Apr 1887 (Baptism, **St. Peter Parish**)

William Free (son):

Residence - 19 Hawthorn Terrace, Church Road - November 9, 1879

39 Lombard Street West - September 23, 1880

1 Brainborough, South Circular Road - October 24, 1882

11 Emor Street - November 25, 1885

1 Emor Street, South Circular Road - April 19, 1887

Occupation - Salesman - November 9, 1879

September 23, 1880

November 25, 1885

Clerk - October 24, 1882

April 19, 1887

Sophia Wyse, daughter of Andrew Wyse (daughter-in-law):

Residence - 84 Rathmines Road - November 9, 1879

Andrew Wyse (father):

Occupation - Druggist

Annesley Free (father):

Occupation - Accountant

Wedding Witnesses:

Andrew Wyse & Richard J. Free

Signatures:

Free Surname Ireland: 1600s to 1900s

- Annesley Free & Anne Free

  o Sarah Florence Free – b. 2 Feb 1874, bapt. 1 May 1874 (Baptism, **St. Mary Parish**)

Annelsey Free (father):

    Residence - 80 Middle Abbey Street - May 1, 1874

    Occupation - Accountant - May 1, 1874

- Arthur Free & Unknown

  o George Free & Catherine O'Neill – 6 Jan 1884 (Marriage, **St. Bride Parish**)

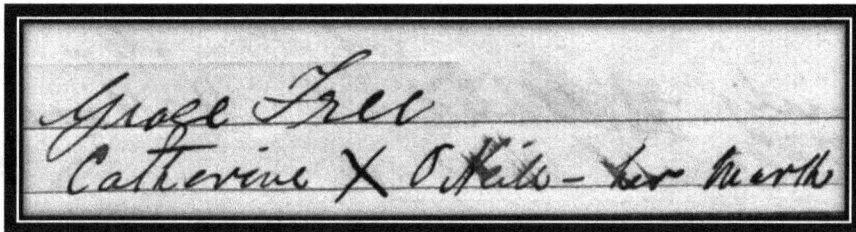

Signatures:

George Free (son):

    Residence - Great Ship Street Barracks - January 6, 1884

    Occupation - Private, West Kent Regiment - January 6, 1884

Catherine O'Neill, daughter of Dennis O'Neill (daughter-in-law):

    Residence - Golden Lane - January 6, 1884

Dennis O'Neill (father):

    Occupation - Laborer

Arthur Free (father):

    Occupation - Laborer

Hurst

Wedding Witnesses:

Agnes Kedey & J. Taylor

Signatures:

- Charles Free & Unknown

  ○ Richard Whitmore Free & Mary Josephine Drury – 17 Oct 1887 (Marriage, **Rathmines Parish**)

    ▪ Richard Whitmore Free – b. 5 Jan 1890, bapt. 20 Apr 1890 (Baptism, **Rathmines Parish**)

Signatures:

Richard Whitmore Free (son):

Residence - 10 Rugby Road - October 17, 1887

14 Rugby Road - April 20, 1890

Occupation - Draper - October 17, 1887

April 20, 1890

Free Surname Ireland: 1600s to 1900s

Mary Josephine Drury, daughter of William Drury (daughter-in-law):

Residence - 1 Sussex Terrace, Mespil Road - October 17, 1887

William Drury (father):

Occupation - Commercial Traveller

Charles Free (father):

Occupation - Farmer

Wedding Witnesses:

Frederick Roe & Elizabeth Roe

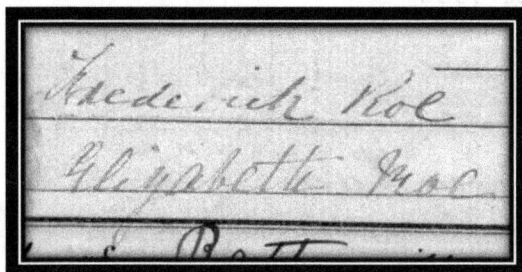

Signatures:

- Edward Free & Elizabeth Unknown
  - Joseph Free – bapt. 1851 (Baptism, St. Andrew Parish (RC))
- George Free & Mary Muldoon
  - Mary Free – b. 8 Mar 1878, bapt. 18 Mar 1878 (Baptism, St. Mary, Pro Cathedral Parish (RC))

George Free (father):

Residence - 8 Old Abbey Street - March 18, 1878

Hurst

- Gulielmo Free & Mary Unknown

  - Mary Anne Free & Thomas Peat – 19 Sep 1880 (Marriage, **St. Agatha Parish (RC)**)

    - Mary Anne Peat – b. 1886, bapt. 1886 (Baptism, **St. Andrew Parish (RC)**)

    - Thomas Patrick Peat – b. 1895, bapt. 1895 (Baptism, **St. Andrew Parish (RC)**)

Mary Anne Free (daughter):

Residence - 13 Ballybough Road - September 19, 1880

Thomas Peat, son of Gulielmo Peat & Bridget Peat (son-in-law):

Residence - 12 Sackville Avenue - September 19, 1880

121 Townsend Street - 1886

1895

Wedding Witnesses:

Michael Murphy & Elizabeth Brennan

- Henry Free & Elizabeth Healy

  - Anne Free & Thomas Thompson – 16 Sep 1873 (Marriage, **St. Catherine Parish (RC)**)

    - Patrick John Thompson – b. 15 Feb 1877, bapt. 19 Feb 1877 (Baptism, **SS. Michael & John Parish (RC)**)

    - Mary Anne Thompson – b. 16 Apr 1880, bapt. 19 Apr 1880 (Baptism, **St. Nicholas Parish (RC)**)

Free Surname Ireland: 1600s to 1900s

Anne Free (daughter):

 Residence - Friar Street - September 16, 1873

Thomas Thompson, son of John Thompson & Margaret Unknown (son-in-law):

 Residence - Friar Street - September 16, 1873

 3 George's Place - February 19, 1877

 31 Plunkett Street - April 19, 1880

Wedding Witnesses:

Daniel Kavanagh & Anne Murphy

- Henry Free & Elizabeth Tighe – 1 Jun 1829 (Marriage, **St. George Parish**)

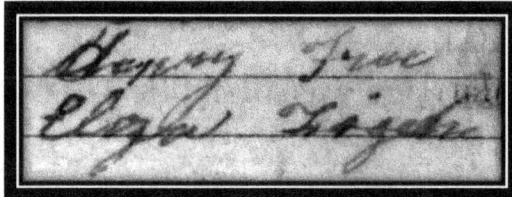

Signatures:

Henry Free (husband):

 Residence - St. George Parish - June 1, 1829

Elizabeth Tighe (wife):

 Residence - St. George Parish - June 1, 1829

Hurst

Wedding Witnesses:

John Hare & Benjamin Ray

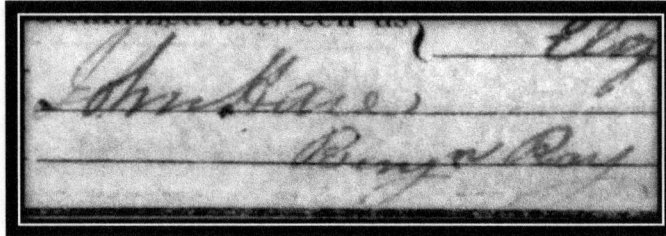

Signatures:

- Henry Free & Mary Delap – 21 Oct 1837 (Marriage, **St. Mary Parish (RC)**)

Mary Delap, daughter of William Delap & Mary Delap (daughter-in-law).

Wedding Witnesses:

William Delap & Mary Delap

- John Free & Eleanor Free
  - Sarah Free – bapt. 23 Oct 1757 (Baptism, **Aghold Parish**)
- John Free & Elizabeth Free
  - Dora Jane Free – b. 14 Feb 1874, bapt. 30 Apr 1874 (Baptism, **St. Peter Parish**)
  - Henry Free – b. 15 Oct 1875, bapt. 21 Nov 1875 (Baptism, **St. Peter Parish**)
  - Edward Free – b. 13 Jan 1878, bapt. 7 Apr 1878 (Baptism, **St. Luke Parish**)

John Free (father):

Residence - Vanies Buildings, Bishop Street - April 30, 1874

4 Bishop Street - November 21, 1875

42 New Row South - April 7, 1878

Free Surname Ireland: 1600s to 1900s

Occupation - Store Keeper - April 30, 1874

Assistant in Store - November 21, 1875

Store Clerk - April 7, 1878

- John Free & Elizabeth McElhone

  o Richard Albert Ernest Free – b. 9 Jun 1884, bapt. 24 Jun 1884 (Baptism, **St. Agatha Parish** (RC))

  o Frederick Oliver Free – b. 30 Sep 1886, bapt. 5 Oct 1886 (Baptism, **St. Agatha Parish** (RC))

  o Elizabeth Maude Free – b. 15 Jan 1889, bapt. 15 Jan 1889 (Baptism, **St. Agatha Parish** (RC))

John Free (father):

Residence - Foster Terrace - June 24, 1884

6 Foster Terrace - October 5, 1886

January 15, 1889

- John Free & Elizabeth O'Brien – 22 Aug 1847 (Marriage, **St. Nicholas Parish** (RC))

Wedding Witnesses:

Joan Larkin & Margaret Dalton

- John Free & Hannah Free

  o John Free – bapt. 18 May 1718 (Baptism, **St. Luke Parish**)

John Free (father):

Residence - Lower Coombe - May 18, 1718

Occupation - Waiter - May 18, 1718

Hurst

- John Free & Jane Hannon

  - Mary Free – b. 1870, bapt. 1896 (Baptism, **Lucan Parish (RC)**)

John Free (father):

Residence - Backerston, Lucan - 1896

- John Free & Jane Unknown

  - James Free – bapt. 1829 (Baptism, **St. Andrew Parish (RC)**)

  - Mary Anne Free – bapt. 1831 (Baptism, **St. Andrew Parish (RC)**)

- John Free & Marcella Fox

  - Anne Free – b. 17 Jan 1883, bapt. 20 Jan 1883 (Baptism, **St. Audoen Parish (RC)**)

John Free (father):

Residence - 4 New Market - January 20, 1883

- John Free & Mary Free

  - Mary Free – bapt. 8 Oct 1751 (Baptism, **Dingle Parish**)

John Free (father):

Occupation - Soldier - October 8, 1751

- John Free & Mary Anne Free

  - Elizabeth Jane Free – bapt. 7 Mar 1824 (Baptism, **Tullow Parish**)

- John Free & Priscilla Unknown

  - Anne Free – b. 27 Jul 1865, bapt. 27 Sep 1867 (Baptism, **St. Catherine Parish**)

  - Henry Free – b. 28 Feb 1867, bapt. 27 Sep 1867 (Baptism, **St. Catherine Parish**), bur. 10 Oct 1867 (Burial, **St. Catherine Parish**)

Free Surname Ireland: 1600s to 1900s

Henry Free (son):

Residence - Brown Street - before October 10, 1867

Age at Death - 7 months

- Jane Free – b. 1 Oct 1868, bapt. 4 Nov 1868 (Baptism, **St. Catherine Parish**)

John Free (father):

Residence - 14 Brown Street - September 27, 1867

November 4, 1868

Occupation - Laborer - September 27, 1867

November 4, 1868

- John Free & Unknown
  - Unknown (Daughter) – bapt. Mar 1733 (Baptism, **Aghold Parish**)

John Free (father):

Residence - Lower Aghold - March 1733

- John Free & Unknown
  - William Free – bapt. 11 Mar 1743 (Baptism, **Aghold Parish**)

Hurst

- John Free & Unknown

  - Hester Free & Benjamin Hopkins – 10 Jan 1850 (Marriage, **St. Catherine Parish**)

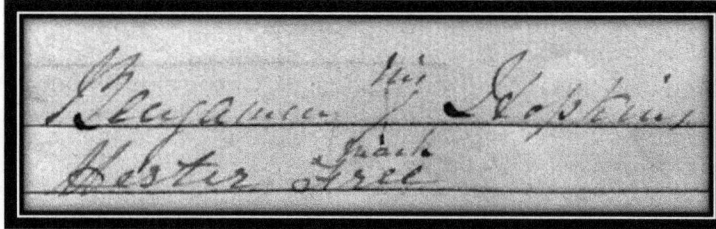

Signatures:

Hester Free (daughter):

  Residence - Sally Place - January 10, 1850

Benjamin Hopkins, son of George Hopkins (son-in-law):

  Residence - Sally Place - January 10, 1850

  Occupation - Carpenter - January 10, 1850

George Hopkins (father):

  Occupation - Farmer

John Free (father):

  Occupation - Farmer

Free Surname Ireland: 1600s to 1900s

Wedding Witnesses:

William Free & Elizabeth Free

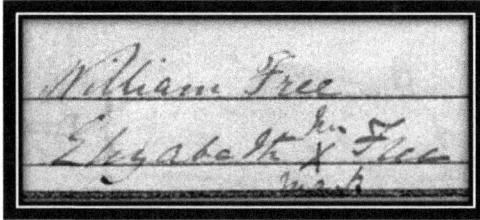

Signatures:

- o William Free (1st Marriage) & Jane Free

  - Hester Free – b. 23 Sep 1849, bapt. 14 Oct 1849 (Baptism, **St. Catherine Parish**)

  - William Free – b. 16 Jan 1852, bapt. 22 Apr 1852 (Baptism, **St. Catherine Parish**)

- o William Free (2nd Marriage) & Anne Woolridge – 1 Apr 1861 (Marriage, **St. Catherine Parish**)

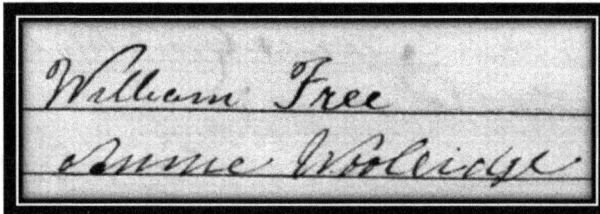

Signatures:

  - William Free, b. 25 Mar 1862, bapt. 18 May 1862 (Baptism, **St. Luke Parish**) & Mary Dwane – 4

    May 1885 (Marriage, **St. Peter Parish**)

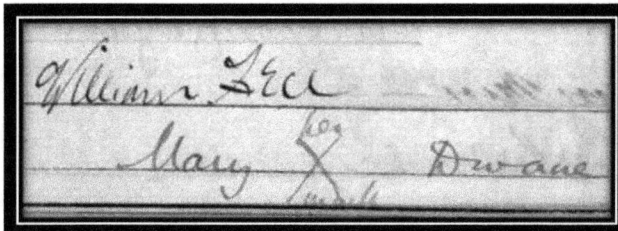

Signatures:

Hurst

William Free (son):

Residence - 11 Shamrock Villas, Harold's Cross - May 4, 1885

Occupation - Porter - May 4, 1885

Mary Dwane, daughter of Edward Dwane (daughter-in-law):

Residence - 67 Rathmines Road - May 4, 1885

Edward Dwane (father):

Occupation - Farmer

William Free (father):

Occupation - Farmer

Wedding Witnesses:

Charles Free & Bridget Dwane

Signatures:

William Free (son):

Residence - Sally Park - October 14, 1849

April 22, 1852

Love Lane - April 22, 1852

April 1, 1861

11 Malpas Street - May 18, 1862

Occupation - Gardener - October 14, 1849

April 22, 1852

April 1, 1861

May 18, 1862

Relationship Status at Marriage - widow

Anne Woolridge, daughter of Richard Woolridge (daughter-in-law):

Residence - Green Villa Avenue - April 1, 1861

Relationship Status at Marriage - minor

Richard Woolridge (father):

Occupation - Farmer

John Free (father):

Occupation - Farmer

Wedding Witnesses:

James Lyons & John Fletcher Free

Signatures:

o John Fletcher Free

Signatures:

- John Free & Unknown

  o Richard Free & Mary Dixon – 7 Jun 1853 (Marriage, **St. Paul Parish**)

Signatures:

- Mary Anne Free – b. 3 Mar 1855, bapt. 3 Jun 1855 (Baptism, **St. Paul Parish**)

- John William Free – b. 29 Oct 1856, bapt. 1 Nov 1857 (Baptism, **St. Nicholas Without Parish**)

Richard Free (son):

Residence - Queen Street - June 7, 1853

45 Queen Street - June 3, 1855

Roper's Rest - November 1, 1857

Free Surname Ireland: 1600s to 1900s

Occupation - Carpenter - June 7, 1853

June 3, 1855

November 1, 1857

Elizabeth Dixon, daughter of Edward Dixon (daughter-in-law):

Residence - Queen Street - June 7, 1853

Occupation - Dress Maker - June 7, 1853

Edward Dixon (father):

Occupation - Wood Sawyer

John Free (father):

Occupation - Farmer

Wedding Witnesses:

James Murphy & Catherine Fox

Signatures:

- John Free & Unknown
  - Anne Free & Dionysius Quirk – 20 Jan 1883 (Marriage, St. Audoen Parish (RC))

Anne Free (daughter):

Residence - 22 Cooke Street - January 20, 1883

Hurst

Dionysius Quirk, son of Patrick Quirk (son-in-law):

Residence - 20 Cook Street - January 20, 1883

Wedding Witnesses:

David Hogan & Alice Flood

- John Free & Unknown
  - Elizabeth Free & Mark Weeks – 5 Sep 1899 (Marriage, **St. Mark Parish**)

Signatures:

Elizabeth Free (daughter):

Residence - 7 Sandwith Place - September 5, 1899

Mark Weeks, son of Mark Weeks (son-in-law):

Residence - 13 Sandwith Terrace, Sandwith Place - September 5, 1899

Occupation - Laborer - September 5, 1899

Mark Weeks (father):

Occupation - Farmer

John Free (father):

Occupation - Laborer

Free Surname Ireland: 1600s to 1900s

Wedding Witnesses:

Elizabeth Browne & Edward Barton

Signatures:

- Joseph Free & Ellen Creighton

  - William Joseph Free – b. 14 Jun 1894, bapt. 29 Jul 1894 (Baptism, **Rathmines Parish**), bapt. 2 Mar 1895 (Baptism, **St. Mary, Donnybrook Parish (RC)**)

Joseph Free (father):

Residence - 10 Smith Cottages - July 29, 1894

10 Smith's Cottages, Marlboro Road - March 2, 1895

Occupation - Private, 8th Hussars - July 29, 1894

- Joshua Free & Catherine Free

  - Anne Free – bur. 18 Jan 1763 (Burial, **Aghold Parish**)

  - Unknown Free – bapt. 25 Feb 1765 (Baptism, **Aghold Parish**)

- Joshua Free & Elizabeth Free

  - Mary Free – bapt. 18 Sep 1757 (Baptism, **Aghold Parish**)

  - Catherine Free – bur. 6 Feb 1761 (Burial, **Aghold Parish**)

Hurst

- Joshua Free & Elizabeth Unknown

  o Joshua Free – b. 4 Mar 1824, bapt. 31 Mar 1824 (Baptism, **St. Peter Parish**), d. 9 Jul 1824, bur. 1824

    (Burial, **St. Peter Parish**)

Joshua Free (son):

Residence - Aungier Street - July 9, 1824

- Peter Free & Sarah Unknown

  o Anne Free – bapt. 26 Sep 1779 (Baptism, **St. Werburgh Parish**)

  o Harriet Free – bapt. 11 Jul 1784 (Baptism, **St. Werburgh Parish**)

Peter Free (father):

Residence - Werburgh Street - September 26, 1779

July 11, 1784

- Richard Free & Anne Adams – 28 May 1844 (Marriage, **Painestown Parish**)

  o Richard Free – b. 4 Apr 1845, bapt. 1 Jun 1845 (Baptism, **Painestown Parish**)

  o Mary Anne Free, b. 26 Aug 1847, bapt. 24 Oct 1847 (Baptism, **Staplestown Parish**) & John Storey

    – 8 Aug 1871 (Marriage, **St. Mark Parish**)

Signatures:

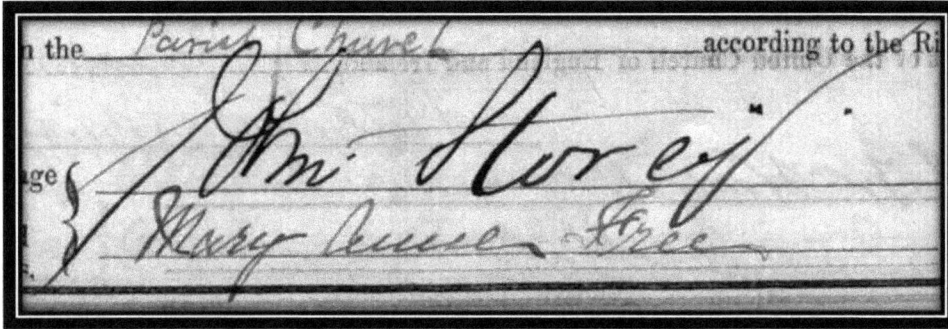

Mary Anne Free (daughter):

    Residence - Great Brunswick Street - August 8, 1871

John Storey, son of John Storey (son-in-law):

    Residence - 12 Creighton Street - August 8, 1871

    Occupation - Master Mariner - August 8, 1871

John Storey (father):

    Occupation - Farmer

Richard Free (father):

    Occupation - Land Steward

Hurst

Wedding Witnesses:

Henry Mason & Frances Storey

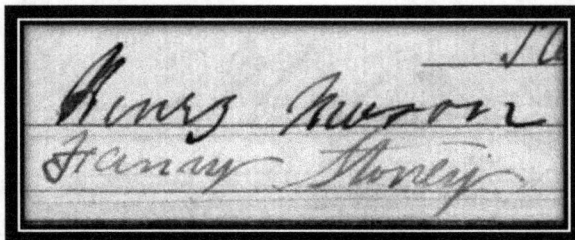

Signatures:

- o Henrietta Free – b. 16 Aug 1849, bapt. 4 Nov 1849 (Baptism, **Staplestown Parish**)

- o Martha Free – bapt. 28 Nov 1852 (Baptism, **Staplestown Parish**)

Richard Free (father):

Residence - Tuiryland - October 24, 1847

November 4, 1849

November 28, 1852

Occupation - Steward - October 24, 1847

November 4, 1849

November 28, 1852

- • Richard Free & Anne Clear – 20 May Unclear (Marriage, **Carlow Parish**)

- • Richard Free & Elizabeth Unknown

  - o Richard Free – b. 8 Apr 1820, bapt. 9 Apr 1820 (Baptism, **St. Catherine Parish**)

Free Surname Ireland: 1600s to 1900s

Richard Free (father):

Residence - Bridge Street - April 9, 1820

- Richard Free & Hester Dowdall – 16 Feb 1751 (Marriage, **Aghold Parish**)
  - o John Free – bur. 26 Apr 1758 (Burial, **Aghold Parish**)
- Robert Free & Unknown
  - o George Free & Anne Doran – 15 Feb 1847 (Marriage, **Tralee Parish**)

Signatures:

George Free (son):

Residence - Killorglin - February 15, 1847

Occupation - Private, 77th Regiment - February 15, 1847

Anne Doran, daughter of Jeremiah Doran (daughter-in-law):

Residence - Tralee - February 15, 1847

Jeremiah Doran (father):

Occupation - Stone Mason

Hurst

Robert Free (father):

    Occupation - Carrier

Wedding Witnesses:

Jeremiah Brennan & Benjamin Carter

Signatures:

- Scott Free & Unknown Free, d. 27 Jan 1836, bur. 1836 (Burial, **St. James Parish**)

Unknown Free (wife):

    Residence - Chamber Street - January 27, 1836

- Thomas Free & Unknown

Signatures:

o Hannah Mary Free & Daniel Walnut Kirwan – 30 Jun 1858 (Marriage, **St. Peter Parish**)

Signature:

Signatures (Marriage):

Hannah Mary Free (daughter):

Residence - 33 Upper Clanbrassil Street - June 30, 1858

Hurst

Daniel Walnut Kirwan, son of Daniel Kirwan (son-in-law):

Residence - 33 Upper Clanbrassil Street - June 30, 1858

Occupation - Gentleman - June 30, 1858

Daniel Kirwan (father):

Occupation - Gentleman

Thomas Free (father):

Occupation - Bricklayer

Wedding Witnesses:

Thomas Free & Abraham Carr

Signatures:

o   Henry Free & Mary Nolan – 2 Oct 1863 (Marriage, **St. Peter Parish**)

Signatures:

Free Surname Ireland: 1600s to 1900s

- Hannah Mary Free – b. 31 Aug 1864, bapt. 14 Dec 1864 (Baptism, **St. Mark Parish**)

- William Henry Free – b. 2 Mar 1866, bapt. 28 Mar 1866 (Baptism, **St. Mark Parish**)

Henry Free (son):

Residence - 36 Power's Court - October 2, 1863

4 Clarence Street - December 14, 1864

3 Harmony Row - March 28, 1866

Occupation - Bricklayer - October 2, 1863

December 14, 1864

March 28, 1866

Mary Nolan, daughter of Owen Nolan (daughter-in-law):

Residence - 22 Herbert Place - October 2, 1863

Occupation - Servant - October 2, 1863

Owen Nolan (father):

Occupation - Gardiner

Thomas Free (father):

Occupation - Bricklayer

Hurst

Wedding Witnesses:

Daniel Walnut Kirwan & Frances Sharpe

Signatures:

- Thomas Free & Unknown
    - Anne Free (1st Marriage) & Unknown Black
    - Anne Free Black (2nd Marriage) & Thomas Clince – 1 Jun 1885 (Marriage, **St. Thomas Parish**)

Signatures:

Anne Free Black (daughter):

Residence - Athol's Hotel & Wexford St. Dublin - June 1, 1885

Relationship Status at Marriage - widow

Thomas Clince, son of Thomas Clince (son-in-law):

Residence - Athol's Hotel &1 Upper Sackville Street - June 1, 1885

Occupation - Castle Dealer - June 1, 1885

Free Surname Ireland: 1600s to 1900s

Thomas Clince (father):

Occupation - Castle Dealer

Thomas Free (father):

Occupation - Farmer

Wedding Witnesses:

William McClelland & George Campbell

Signatures:

- Unknown Free & Mary Free

  o John Free – b. 1890, bapt. 20 Aug 1893 (Baptism, **St. George Parish**)

Mary Free (mother):

Residence - 64 Eccles Street - August 20, 1893

- Unknown Free & Unknown

  o Richard Free

Signature:

Hurst

- Unknown Free & Unknown

  o Richard Free

Signature:

- Unknown Free & Unknown

  o Richard Free

Signature:

- Unknown Free & Unknown

  o Sophia Free

Signature:

- Unknown Free & Unknown

  o Thomas Free

Signature:

Free Surname Ireland: 1600s to 1900s

- William Free & Agnes Frazer

  - William Free – b. 1866, bapt. 1866 (Baptism, **St. Mary Parish (RC)**)

- William Free & Anne Free

  - David Free – b. 29 Jul 1879, bapt. 25 Jan 1880 (Baptism, **Rathmines Parish**)

William Free (father):

Residence - 16 Duggan Place - January 25, 1880

Occupation - Laborer - January 25, 1880

- William Free & Unknown

  - Richard Free & Elizabeth Bayle – 23 May 1870 (Marriage, **Cloydagh Parish**)

Signatures:

Richard Free (son):

Residence - Shurle Union of Cloydagh - May 23, 1870

Occupation - Laborer - May 23, 1870

Elizabeth Bayle, daughter of Thomas Bayle (daughter-in-law):

Residence - Kelvin Groves, Carlow - May 23, 1870

Occupation - Servant - May 23, 1870

Hurst

Thomas Bayle (father):

    Occupation - Steward

William Free (father):

    Occupation - Steward

Wedding Witnesses:

Henry Erett & Mary Larkin

Signatures:

Individual Baptisms/Births

None Were Listed

Individual Burials

- Anne Free – bur. 8 Nov 1732 (Burial, **St. Paul Parish**)

Anne Free (deceased):

Age at Death - child

- Daniel Free – bur. 27 Mar 1740 (Burial, **St. Paul Parish**)

Daniel Free (deceased):

Age at Death - child

- Edward Free – b. Feb 1878, bur. 24 Apr 1879 (Burial, **St. Peter Parish**)

Edward Free (deceased):

Residence - 18 Williams Place - before April 24, 1879

Age at Death - 15 months

- Henry Free – d. 10 Oct 1867, bur. 1867 (Burial, **St. Catherine Parish (RC)**)

Henry Free (deceased):

Residence - Brown Street - October 10, 1867

- Jacob Free – bur. 17 Dec 1728 (Burial, **St. Nicholas Without Parish**)

Free Surname Ireland: 1600s to 1900s

- John Free – bur. 18 Nov 1732 (Burial, **St. Paul Parish**)

John Free (deceased):

    Age at Death - child

- Margaret Free – bur. 1 Mar 1829 (Burial, **St. Mary Parish**)

Margaret Free (deceased):

    Residence - Widow's House, Britain Street - before March 1, 1829

- Mary Free – bur. 8 Sep 1721 (Burial, **St. Paul Parish**)
- Mary Jane Free – d. 7 Apr 1855, bur. 1855 (Burial, **Clondalkin Parish**)

Mary Jane Free (deceased):

    Residence - Cheeverstown - April 7, 1855

- Mary Josephine Free – b. 1867, d. 16 Mar 1898, bur. 1898 (Burial, **Clondalkin Parish**)

Mary Josephine Free (deceased):

    Residence - Claremount, Clondalkin - March 16, 1898

    Age at Death - 31 years

- Matthew Free – b. 1883, bur. 26 Feb 1888 (Burial, **Aghold Parish**)

Matthew Free (deceased):

    Residence - Coolkenno - before February 26, 1888

    Age at Death - 5 years

Hurst

- Richard Free – b. 1819, bur. 12 Nov 1884 (Burial, **Staplestown Parish**)

Richard Free (deceased):

    Residence - Moyle - before November 12, 1884

    Age at Death - 65 years

- Unknown Free – bur. 19 Oct 1835 (Burial, **Tralee Parish**)

Individual Marriages

- Anne Free & Peter Bracken

  o Mary Bracken – b. 2 Jul 1863, bapt. 10 Jul 1863 (Baptism, **St. Nicholas Parish** (RC))

  o Anne Bracken – b. 25 Jul 1869, bapt. 6 Aug 1869 (Baptism, **St. Michan Parish** (RC))

Peter Bracken (father):

Residence - Handkerchief Alley - July 10, 1863

57 Mary's Lane - August 6, 1869

- Catherine Free & James Maher

  o John Maher – bapt. 8 Jan 1817 (Baptism, **St. Nicholas Parish** (RC))

- Catherine Free & James Mara – 20 Aug 1808 (Marriage, **St. Andrew Parish** (RC))

Wedding Witnesses:

James Magee & Anne Magee

- Elizabeth Free & Lawrence Farrell

  o William Farrell – b. 1879, bapt. 1879 (Baptism, **St. Andrew Parish** (RC))

  o Margaret Farrell – b. 1881, bapt. 1881 (Baptism, **St. Andrew Parish** (RC))

  o Elizabeth Farrell – b. 1883, bapt. 1883 (Baptism, **St. Andrew Parish** (RC))

  o Mary Anne Farrell – b. 1886, bapt. 1886 (Baptism, **St. Andrew Parish** (RC))

Hurst

Lawrence Farrell (father):

Residence - 4 Mark's Court - 1879

9 Sandwith Lane - 1881

1883

16 Sandwith Place - 1886

- Elizabeth Free & Thomas Hickey

  o Emily Hickey – b. 1 Sep 1858, bapt. 15 Sep 1858 (Baptism, **St. Michan Parish (RC)**)

Thomas Hickey (father):

Residence - Lying Inn from Dispensary Lane - September 15, 1858

- Elizabeth Free & Thomas Moody – 1 Dec 1713 (Marriage, **Aghold Parish**)
- Frances Free & Thomas Flood – 12 Jun 1848 (Marriage, **St. Mary, Pro Cathedral Parish (RC)**)

Wedding Witnesses:

John Keogh & Michael Molloy

- Margaret Free & William Portway

  o William Charles Portway – b. 10 Dec 1884, bapt. 23 Jan 1885 (Baptism, **Rathmines Parish (RC)**)

William Portway (father):

Residence - Portobello Barrack - January 23, 1885

Free Surname Ireland: 1600s to 1900s

- Mary Free & John Dowdall – 28 Oct 1742 (Marriage, **Aghold Parish**)

- Mary Free & Stephen Campbell

  o Peter Campbell – b. 13 Oct 1856, bapt. 24 Oct 1856 (Baptism, **St. Nicholas Parish** (RC))

Stephen Campbell (father):

Residence - 43 Golden Lane - October 24, 1856

Name Variations

Includes Latin and Abbreviated forms of names found in the original documents.

Abigail = Abigale, Abigall

Anne = Ann, Anna, Annae

Bartholomew = Barth, Bartholmeus, Bartholomeo

Bridget = Birgis, Brigid, Brigida, Bridgit

Catherine = Catharine, Catharina, Catharinae, Catherina, Cath, Catha, Cathae, Cathe, Cathn, Kate

Charles = Carolus, Charls, Chas

Christopher = Christoph

Daniel = Danielem, Danielis

Edmund = Edmond

Edward = Ed, Edwd

Eleanor = Eleo, Eleonora, Elinor, Ellenor

Elizabeth = Betty, Elisa, Elisabeth, Eliz, Eliza, Elizab, Elizh, Elizth

Ellen = Elena, Ellena

Emily = Emilia

Esther = Essie, Ester

Francis = Fransicum

George = Geo, Georg, Georgius

Grace = Gratiae

Gulielmo = Guil, Guillelmi, Gulielmum, Guillelmus, Gulmi

Helen = Helena

Free Surname Ireland: 1600s to 1900s

Honor = Hanora, Honora

James = Jacobi, Jacobus, Jas

Jane = Joanna

Jeanne = Jeannae, Joannae

Joan = Johanna, Joney

John = Jno, Joannem, Joannes, Johannis

Joseph = Jos

Juliana = Julian

Leticia = Letitia, Lettice, Letticia

Lewis = Louis

Luke = Lucas

Margaret = Margarita, Margaritae, Margeret, Marget, Margt

Martha = Marthae

Mary = Maria, My

Mary Anne = Marianna, Marianne, Maryanne

Michael = Michaelis, Michl

Patrick = Pat, Patt, Patk, Patricii, Patricius

Peter = Petri

Richard = Ricardi, Ricardus, Rich, Richd

Robert = Roberti

Rose = Rosa, Rosae

Thomas = Thom, Thomae, Thoms, Thos, Ths

Timothy = Timotheus, Timy

William = Wil, Will, Willm, Wm

Notes

Notes

Notes

Notes

Notes

Notes

Index

Free Surname Ireland: 1600s to 1900s

F

Farrell

Baptisms

Elizabeth
1883 37

Margaret
1881 37

Mary Anne
1886 37

William
1879 37

Births

Elizabeth
1883 37

Margaret
1881 37

Mary Anne
1886 37

William
1879 37

Lawrence 37

Flood

Thomas 38

Fox

Marcella 10

Frazer

Agnes 31

Free

Baptisms

Anne
1779 Sep 26 20
1865 Sep 27 10
1883 Jan 20 10

Annesley Hamilton
1880 Sep 23 1

Charlotte Mary
1882 Oct 24 1

David
1880 Jan 25 31

Dora Jane
1874 Apr 30 8

Edward
1878 Apr 7 8

Elizabeth Jane
1824 Mar 7 10

Elizabeth Maude
1889 Jan 15 9

Frederick Oliver
1886 Oct 5 9

Hannah Mary
1864 Dec 14 27

Harriet
1784 Jul 11 20

Henrietta
1849 Nov 4 22

Henry
1867 Sep 27 10
1875 Nov 21 8

Hester
1849 Oct 14 13

James
1829 10

Jane
1868 Nov 4 11

John
1718 May 18 9
1893 Aug 20 29

John William
1857 Nov 1 16

Joseph
1851 5

Joshua
1824 Mar 31 20

Martha
1852 Nov 28 22

Mary
1751 Oct 8 10
1757 Sep 18 19
1878 Mar 18 5
1896 10

Mary Anne
1831 10
1847 Oct 24 20
1855 Jun 3 16

Richard

49

About The Author

Donovan Hurst graduated from San Diego State University with a Bachelor of Arts in the major field of studies of History and a minor in the field of studies of Anthropology. He is a current member of The General Society of Mayflower Descendants and has been conducting genealogical research for over 10 years tracing back his ancestors to their ancestral homelands in Denmark, England, France, Germany, Ireland, Norway, and Scotland.

www.ingramcontent.com/pod-product-compliance
Lightning Source LLC
Chambersburg PA
CBHW081201270326
41930CB00014B/3253